Poetic and Philosophical Reflections on Economic Development

Donald T. Iannone

WISDOM WORK PRESS

Cleveland, Ohio

At Wisdom Work Press, we define wisdom as the conscious integration of knowledge, experience, reflective understanding, and a measured tolerance for life's uncertainties and its continuous changes. Personal wisdom is most important, which requires self-knowledge, discipline, and self-leadership. These qualities ensure that we walk the wisdom path through life. Our publications and services help others to discover and mount their wisdom path in life.

Website: https://wisdomworkpress.wordpress.com/

Poetic and Philosophical Reflections on Economic Development

ISBN-13: 978-1534676510
ISBN-10: 1534676511

Poetic and Philosophical Reflections on Economic Development

DEDICATION

Poetic and Philosophical Reflections on Economic Development is dedicated to the men and women working as economic developers across America and the rest of the world. Your work is important to society, and your success in creating greater broad-based prosperity in the future can be accelerated by a deeper dive into the philosophical issues encountered in practicing economic development. Philosophy matters, and poetry is a powerful vehicle for communicating philosophical ideas, as this small book hopefully shows us.

Don Iannone
Cleveland, Ohio
August 26, 2016

TABLE OF CONTENTS

FOREWORD

"The job to be done in philosophy is really more a job on oneself. On one's own viewpoint. On how one sees things. ~Ludwig Wittgenstein

This is a self-help book. I wrote it to clarify my personal philosophy of economic development. I used poetry to explore these philosophical issues because poetry is deeply personal. What is personal is most sacred. What is most sacred is buried deep in our hearts. In poetry, there is no avoiding what lies in our hearts. Likewise, philosophy is intensely personal. If you don't believe me, look at the hardcore philosophical issues being debated with great emotion by Americans in this year's presidential race.

Economic development is the painstaking work of growing and sustaining good jobs, prosperity, and economic vitality in communities in a turbulent, conflicted, and uncertain world. It is not for the faint of heart. Competition for wealth and power in communities is brutal, and getting people to work together requires shared understanding, negotiation, compromise, and a deep-seated will and commitment to learn and grow together. That said, economic development is rewarding work.

While a great deal of good exists in the world, it is sometimes offset by greed, abuse of power, extremism, fear, prejudice, and selfish pride. We must rebalance the scales in favor of the good over these offsetting challenges, build a sense of common purpose, and help each other grow wiser, stronger, more caring, and resilient in the face of rampant change. We can achieve this if we work to understand ourselves and others, and build upon what connects us rather than what pulls us apart. This book provides insights on how to do this.

I share this small book with you, hoping you will join me on the journey of self-understanding to make the world a better place. That is why I work in economic development and why I write poetry.

Don Iannone
Cleveland, Ohio
August 26, 2016

Sailing the Economic Development Seas for Forty Years

It's gone before you know it—Your career, even your life.
Forty years in economic development—Now a long stream of
consciousness of people, events, and places—
Memories flashing back in bits and pieces,
becoming poetic verses and storylines.

There were bruises—Crashing hard on the beaches
of good intention—Well-meaning goals shipwrecked
by nearsighted captains, unforeseen storms and high winds,
and on occasion Titanic-sinking icebergs.
I survived—Miraculously a lifeboat usually within reach.

I remember most the great sunrises and sunsets—Special times
when development projects worked out, and when
beautiful new opportunities took shape on the horizon.
And silly things that brought colleagues and friends together—
For one, Bud Light chair races at EDI Norman in the early '90s.

When things get rough, we all pray for safe harbors—
Protected places where our spirits rejuvenate in laughter.
But no good economic developer stays there for long—
We're all warriors in search of the next challenge
that makes us stronger and helps us feel more alive.

I loved the human pyramids—Those memorable times when
people worked together, climbed higher, and touched the stars.
It's great to see ED blossom into a profession— To watch
old sailors turn over the wheel to the younger ones, and
see economic development embrace diversity and change.

The ship's GPS says nothing but change ahead—
Fair skies and smooth sailing, and our share of stormy seas
and gale force winds, forcing us to pay close watch.
All and all, economic developers will grow stronger—
A very good sign for the places and people they serve.

Less Structure and More Flow in Economic Development

We should think more about processes—That is the animating
forces that create motion in economic development,
and less about structures—Walls and other temporary things
we build to keep the world from changing.

Visualize economic development as having a soul—An underlying
energy field flowing through everything economic developers do.
Harnessing and channeling this energy is our main job—Giving
life to communities, businesses, jobs and more.

When this energy stops flowing, in the form of money, ideas,
innovations, markets, compassion, and creativity, we die.
That's why economic developers are needed—To act as economic
Reiki masters, removing the blocks, and keeping things flowing.

Wealth forms where life energy flows—In places, businesses, and
people, who are open to being alive and willing to grow.
Communities get left behind when they have too many old
structures that constipate prosperity and wealth formation.

The incentives of the future will be economic laxatives that loosen
up communities, ridding them of negative economic energy, and
helping the positive economic energy to flow more freely,
take new form, and birth new vital opportunities.

Jobs in the future will be self-renewing—No need for training
and workforce development as we know it today.
And businesses will be energy centers—Pulsating products and
services with perfect timing into world markets.

Communities will self-regulate to remain in synch
with what they need and what the universe demands of them.
It's all about keeping life energy flowing—Makes me glad I
completed my third-degree Reiki Master training last year.

The Invisible Hand and the Soul of Economic Development

Adam Smith was a religious man—
An 18th century moral philosopher no less.
Though often misunderstood and misused,
Adam Smith's "Invisible Hand" has become a centering idea
among economists and economic tinkers alike.

I wonder if Adam Smith would approve of the idea
that economic development has a soul—Something higher
that demands to be expressed in development projects.
Something that transcends the egos carved into buildings,
businesses, and communities by the rich and powerful.

Surely an elegant idea—poetic in many respects,
the Invisible Hand is a thing of beauty, in that
it seeks to explain a lot with a little.
But does this hand act alone, or
does some other invisible force guide it?

The Invisible Hand never acts alone—
The heart, for both good and bad cause,
guides the hand, and even deeper,
the soul gives presence to what develops in the name
of economic development in communities.

$1.00 Tacos

Driving to work this morning,
I noticed three bars within a mile of each another
sporting signs advertising $1.00 tacos.

At first, I thought this was strange, but then I remembered
that was precisely what the free market is all about—
Giving consumers what they want, even $1.00 tacos.

Upon reflection, I wondered why there was no price competition,
or at least some proclaimed differentiation of the product, but
maybe a taco isn't a taco isn't a taco.

Then I realized what was really going on—The soul of economic
development was at work: The tacos were merely an incentive,
enticing thirsty customers to stop in and buy drinks.

After all, bars make money selling drinks, not tacos.

Immediate Openings: Full-Time Positions on All Shifts!

Start at $10.00 to $11.00 per hour.
Weekly paycheck.
Great management—
We take care of our people!
Safe work environment.

Worksite requirements:
Must be at least 18 years of age.
Able to lift at least 50 pounds.
Able to stand for shift duration.
Pass drug test and background check.

Apply online today: www.deadendjobs.com

Now Auditioning the Class of 2016

With no disrespect to women,
I write this poem, calling attention to
the less than desirable labor market realities
that sometimes prey upon women.

Are you a recent female high school graduate,
who is at least eighteen years old,
fit, attractive, outgoing personality, and
driven by creative self-expression?

If so, we offer high-paying jobs, with
intensive on-the-job training, along with
a generous work clothing allowance, and
a safe and entertaining work environment.

Our professional clientele appreciates creativity, and
our performing artists earn $500.00 or more per night.
Call Floyd at Pandemonium Gentlemen's Club
for a personal interview: 888-624-8054.

An Editorial on the Proposed Outdoor Bowling Alley in Downtown Zappa Wazoo

New ideas dance the line between genius and insanity.
Where does an outdoor bowling alley along Main Street
in Downtown Zappa Wazoo fall along that line?

Roll a bowling ball down some downtown streets at high noon
and you wouldn't hit a single person—
So why not build an outdoor bowling alley on Main Street?

Cities need new ideas to survive and grow,
including transformational ideas, or those
upsetting the proverbial apple cart with a bowling ball.

History is littered with geniuses—
Many of whom were thought to be crazy.
Listen to your crazies!

As for an outdoor bowling alley on Main Street—
Why not?
Bowling could be right up Zappa Wazoo's alley!

Payday Lenders

Payday lenders outnumber Starbucks and McDonalds combined!
Now that is a growth industry, but not one
on most economic developers' business attraction lists.

What's the impetus for payday lenders' growth?
Large numbers of desperate people, trying to make ends meet,
even if that means paying 400% annual interest rates.

Payday lenders are everywhere—Rundown strip shopping centers,
the lowliest and seediest downtown streets, and even
outside the gates of the local military base.

Financially-challenged people are everywhere, and
some with poor credit scores are willing to risk
their car or house for a fist full of grimy dollar bills.

Payday lenders are reminders—that a growing number
of people live in economic desperation, and
at times the cure is worse than the disease itself.

Fairness in Economic Development

What is fair in economic development?
Following the rules is one way to judge fairness.
Do we agree on which rules should be followed
in the pursuit of economic development, and
do we intend that everyone follow the same rules?

Justice is another avenue for judging fairness.
The heart of justice for many is giving due regard
to one's own and others' rights and interests.
Do we agree on which rights and interests should be regarded
as we weigh fairness in economic development?

The principle of equity says fairness is defined by input, or
what people contribute or produce, and that fair treatment is
a matter of giving people what they deserve.
Do we agree on which inputs should be considered
in defining fairness in economic development?

Some look to the principle of equality to judge fairness, but
how do we handle the issue that justice may require the unequal
treatment of unequals, which undermines equality?
Do we agree egalitarianism produces fairness, and
benefits and burdens should be distributed equally?

As a start, let's ponder the rules we should follow,
the rights and interests we should consider,
how we decide what stakeholders deserve,
whether benefits and burdens should be distributed equally, and
what will bring about greater fairness in economic development.

The Millwright Poet

Millwrights install and repair machinery in factories—
That was Dad's job for many years, and
before he went to work each morning, he wrote poems on
lined and unlined paper, rumpled scraps of paper, and
occasionally on napkins and paper towels.
Dad was a millwright poet.

Dad knew good poems from bad ones because
he knew good poems hum like well-maintained machines.
If the poem didn't hum, Dad tinkered with it until it did.
One day I asked Dad for guidance on how to write good poems.
His advice? Always write poetry with a pencil and a large eraser
because revision is the secret to writing good poems.

Dad's advice pointed up his understanding of how all things,
including poetry and a millwright's work, are connected.
He also knew that life was never perfect, and
it is all about making the right changes until things hum, and
that hum is the universe telling us "We have done what we can do,
and now let's be satisfied with what we've accomplished."

Poetry was a spiritually centering aspect of Dad's life, and
while my poetry is different than my father's,
poetry plays the same centering role in my life.
Over time, I have come to discover poetry's power in carrying us
to magical places, including encounters with our very souls.

All this begs the question: Was my Dad a millwright
who wrote poetry, or was he a poet
who repaired factory machinery?
Similarly, am I an economic developer who writes poetry, or
I am a poet who works to strengthen local economies?
The answer is: Everything we do is a part of our life's work.

Postscript:

After writing this poem, I searched the Internet to determine if any other millwright poets existed. To my chagrin, I discovered "The Millwright Poet," an interview video of D. J. De Pree, the founder of Herman Miller, a highly successful furniture company in Zeeland, Michigan. During the interview, De Pree talked about the company's millwright in the 1920s, who died suddenly. In speaking with the millwright's wife, De Pree discovered the millwright was a poet. This discovery shocked De Pree, leading him to ponder the exact same question I did in writing this poem about my Dad: "Was he a poet who did millwright's work, or was he a millwright who wrote poetry?" From that experience, Mr. De Pree realized that each of us is extraordinary, and we bring unique gifts to life. This incident radically changed how De Pree viewed his workforce and its value to Herman Miller.

Flowering Business Start-Ups

It's a beautiful thing
to watch new businesses start-up,
like colorful tulips and roses,
taking root, and
sprouting in a late spring garden.

It's important to start with hardy seeds,
planted carefully in the right places, and
then watered,
given enough sun, and
kept free of strangling weeds.

Not all seeds birth flowers, and
not all business start-ups survive and grow
into thriving companies, which is why
we must plant the right seeds in the right places,
and ensure they have what they need to grow.

Good Jobs

A good job engages the body, mind and spirit.
It does so in a balanced way,
helping the worker and the world grow stronger
in an integrated way.

A good job adds benefit—
both material and nonmaterial in nature
to the worker and the world, helping
each to become better.

A good job produces more value
than it consumes, and
it is adaptable to change
to stay in tune with the times.

A good job is about meaning and purpose—
the deeper things we seek in life, and most of all
it must align with our personal calling—
that special reason we were put here in the first place.

Let's work at creating more good jobs.
In doing so, economic developers are fulfilling
their deepest calling—
breathing new economic life into communities.

The Smiling Man in the Employment Line

He impressed me—
the way he smiled,
as he stood with the other hungry faces,
with vacant downcast eyes, wearing
worn defeated shoes with no laces—
Shoes two sizes bigger than their feet.
His smile, a sunbeam,
spread across his broad whiskered face.
His determination gleamed through
his faded blue work shirt, all the way down
to his large muscular hands, that weren't afraid
of a sweat-stained shovel handle, or
to grip the sour-smelling rags, used to clean
the public toilets at the train station.
I counted them—133 men and 41 women, waiting
to be chosen for work, any job
that would pay them a dime, perhaps a quarter.
Enough for a loaf of day-old bread, maybe some beans.
If lucky, a can of oily sardines.
I was glad they picked him.
His smile would give hope to others,
encouraging them not to give up.
Each deserved a job,
some food for their families,
a pair of shoes that fits, and
most of all, a chance to smile again.

Note: This poem is based upon a story my father told me when I was
a young boy. It is about the Great Depression years.

Wall Street and Main Street Economic Development

Wall Street is but a tiny 0.7-mile-long street, running
eight blocks, northwest to southeast in Lower Manhattan.
Home to the stock market, whose perpetual ups and downs
impact every community across America's 3.8 million mile² area.
Small place, gargantuan impact.
The epicenter of financial revolutions.

A fabled place of silver spoons and golden parachutes.
The dark den of cut-throat capitalism, allowing
the nation's top 1% to gain control of 42% of its wealth.
The trading hub for the rich and powerful, rolling the dice,
hedging their bets, wresting control
of the world's largest corporations and governments.

Through its intricate web, Wall Street has a great deal to say
about Main Street economic development, and
whether businesses and communities grow or die.
It is the vortex of job creation and destruction—
deciding the world's economic winners and losers.
Friend or foe,
Wall Street is part of economic development's soul.

As the Great Recession Begins

Times have gotten pretty tough
Perhaps a diamond in the rough
Everyone feeling the pain
As the economy raises Cain.

Working hard, no guarantee
Retirements washed out to sea
Rich and poor, both are losing
As the markets take a bruising.

Makes you wonder, when it'll end
Empty wallets, blowing in the wind
Leaner times, here to stay
Easy money, not today.

Easy to point a finger of blame
Don't forget, we all played the game
Living way beyond our means
Now we're eating pork and beans.

Lessons abound for everyone
Change ahead, won't be fun
Go back to things that matter
Steer clear, all the idle chatter.

Let's re-envision the American Dream
It's a busted old and tired machine
Let's fix the planet, you and me
If I'm right, it'll set us free.

Note: Written at the onset of the Great Recession in December 2007.

Small is Beautiful

Small is beautiful, says E. F. Schumacher,
a self-proclaimed Buddhist economist, and
longstanding sustainability advocate.
His vision? Growing bigger isn't the end game
in economics and economic development.

The world needs a new balance—
One grounded in quality, not quantity, and
one we can support long-term,
without mortgaging our futures.
It starts with a new vision. What's yours?

Brexit, the Morning After

Leave they said!
By a narrow margin, British voters
cast ballots to leave the EU.
With the vote just behind us,
people around the world are wondering
whether leaving is the right thing to do.

Brexit points up the growing angst in the world
over income inequality, immigration, security,
freedom and self-determination, and
the deeper, more visceral issue of what's fair.
If the vote sprouts legs, many tough decisions will arise—
few of which I fear we are ready to handle with wisdom.

If we're willing, we can learn from this vote—
that all of us are connected by something deeper—
that is by the very river of life, flowing through us,
carrying us in new unforeseen directions.
Blessed be the tie that binds—It's not enough to save ourselves,
also we must work to save each other.

The Many Hats of the Economic Developer

Deal-maker
tie breaker
   strategist-planner
   boundary spanner
     tightrope walker
     fast talker
       gamekeeper
       peace keeper
        magician
        politician
          community leader
          business seeder
            negotiator
            job creator
              gatekeeper
              minesweeper
            collaborator
            site locator
          alchemist
          optimist
       thought leader
       mind reader
     investor
     court jester
   stuntman
   front man
     architect-builder
     opportunity filter
       coach-mentor
       economic epicenter
          firefighter
          speech writer
             job creator
             place-maker
               romanticizer
               at times poetizer

Urban Rebirth

Life seemed a far-off place in the city—
A forgotten land of gravestones, lost planets.
A barren dejected wasteland without memories.
Then one day, without provocation,
sunshine fell upon the land, and
clusters of boorish weeds began to grow in the field.

After a long period of bemused intercourse,
the weeds birthed a timid yellow wildflower,
whose sweet scent attracted the attention of a large bumblebee,
whose torn forewing caused the maimed creature
to fly off-course into the forgotten field of weeds.
It was love at first sight.

As more flowers began to grow,
a small cabbage butterfly spotted the field,
and after many abbreviated visits,
the field soon became its home.
Other bees and butterflies migrated to the field
in search of food and companionship.

The barren wasteland has surrendered—
Given itself over to life.
Greens have replaced the browns.
Flowers now outnumber the weeds.
Butterflies, bees, and other creatures live
in large numbers amidst the colorful flowers.
A new thriving metropolis now stands
where once only brownfields pined for love.

Uptown Martins Ferry

Uptown Martins Ferry.
A place I cherished growing up.
Almost gone today—
Shame on us for shopping at Walmart!

As a boy, economic development meant nothing to me,
but I did know the importance
of sitting at the Woolworth's lunch counter and
sipping cherry-flavored sodas with good friends.

Ten-year old boys are more prone to spend money than save it.
Only because Uncle Hank opened my Christmas Club account
at the Uptown Peoples Savings Bank,
I learned the importance of financial planning in life.

We learned about the world at the Uptown library—
Filled with maps, encyclopedias, novels, and old photographs—
Words and images fueling our imaginations, and
giving us the courage to become world explorers.

As a young boy, I knew in my heart
that Uptown was the center of the universe—
More than just a place to shop. It was the garden
where lifelong friendships and memories grow.

Uptown's empty stores, now filled with faded memories—
But let us never forget the movies at Fenray Theater,
Skyscraper ice cream cones at Islay's, and
buying baseball cards with friends at Tidbits variety store.

The Fairy Tale About Things Getting Better

Lincoln didn't free the slaves for long—
they work for 21st century corporate plantations,
breaking their backs, selling their brains for the almighty dollar.

Workers continue to be exploited,
worked to death, and
thrown to their graves.

Job security, a perverse fairy tale.
Retirement, a carrot waved over our heads,
convincing us to work longer and harder.

Things aren't getting better for most—
We have the ludicrously rich, and abhorrently poor.
Not much different than a century and a half ago.

New-Age, Old-Age Parks

First we built industrial parks,
then business office parks,
then university research parks, and now
because we're living so much longer,
we're building new-age, old-age parks.

Not geriatric warehouses,
rather high-tech fountains of youth.
Alive communities,
steeped in nature, wisdom, creativity, and
overflowing with life.

No turning back the hands of time, but
plenty of time on our hands
to create longer and richer lives—
someday well past one hundred and twenty—
Yet a new normal enters our lives.

Economic Development and the Middle Way

Forget the middle class—it's passé
Concentrate on the Middle Way
Avoid cataclysmic extremes
Birth new economic dreams.

Break out of the rich-poor box
Transcend the duality paradox
Create jobs that truly matter
A fairer economic ladder.

This is what the Buddha taught
The Middle Way, the right spot
No need for extreme market swings
A new economy in the wings.

Here's your new lodestone
Learn from this old koan
Right and left to the center
Leave room for any and all to enter.

When a Factory's Life Ends

Foul gray smoke once belched
from the tall red brick chimneys.
A bittersweet sign of life—
when the old factory was still working.
The smoke has now ended,
along with the noisy metal-banging
that kept men busy
from sun up till sundown.
The iron gates are chained shut.
Never again will they greet the dark faces
of hardened men with stale breath
from strong black coffee and cigarettes.
Too easy to blame the wildcat strikes
for the factory's foreboding silence,
but hungry workers elsewhere, willing
to work for much less,
and customers needing less metal,
are just as much the reason why
the dark faces have grown much darker.
The mill is history—
a cold, lifeless archaeological ruin.
So are the paychecks that paid the bills,
giving small consolation to the two thousand men
laughing at each other's lame jokes,
dreaming of days they wouldn't have to work so hard.
Now that day has come, and
both their dreams and jokes have come to an end.

5 Things Everyone Should Know About Economic Developers

Economic developers are human,
just like you and me.
Don't expect miracles from them, and
don't put them on pedestals, like
invincible gunslingers and fabled folk heroes.

Economic developers must balance
the interests and needs of businesses and communities
in developing local economies, and they must work
in line with short and longer term realities.
This balance requires constant attention.

Economic developers must serve the interests of democracy, and
at any cost avoid the pitfalls of autocracy and aristocracy.
For this reason, economic developers must be committed
to advancing broad-based prosperity and the common good
through productive and inclusive growth.

Economic developers need your help in strengthening jobs,
community, and prosperity, and for that reason, they need for
everyone to do their part in competing for new opportunities.
When you see a good development idea, support it, and
be a part of the solution, when economic problems come your way.

And finally, accept that economic development realities
always exists somewhere between opinions and facts,
microscopes and telescopes,
courage and fear,
and what's good for today and tomorrow.

Philosophy Matters in Economic Development

Philosophy matters in economic development—
That is what we believe about the nature of reality.
Ethical dilemmas lurk around every corner,
especially when we face hard choices
about how to use scarce resources, and
who benefits most from the commonwealth's seeds.

Don't sweep the hard questions under the rug, and
don't pretend wealth and power have nothing to do
with whose goals and dreams are pursued.
Test your ideas in the mirror of truth, but first
give definition to your meaning of truth, and
how it compares to others.

Discipline your thoughts, and
don't be afraid to question everything—
For surely your thoughts will grow stronger
in the presence of hard questions.
And don't ignore the face of uncertainty, staring
back at us in each moment of decision and choice.

With each development thesis offered, ask yourself
if an antithesis also exists, and once you see
the many sides of reality, search for the synthesis
bringing disparate pieces together, and don't rush to action
just because you want to assert your will upon others.
For reality always exists beyond what we will.

Be careful when you decide to use the god card—
Because your god just may work for another.
Understand the science of things,
but don't for a moment believe
that science isn't human, and
that scientists are any different than priests.

Philosophy matters in economic development—
What is your definition of reality?

Elmira

For a short time, I worked in Elmira as a consultant
to Southern Tier Economic Growth, aka STEG.
My job was to look ahead, five to ten years out, and
help local leaders decide in which baskets to put their eggs,
that is which economic opportunities should be grown
to spark greater prosperity in New York's Southern Tier.

History is revealing in future pathfinding, like the origin of a place's
name, or how a river city learns to dance at the water's edge.
I discovered Elmira was named after Phoebe Elmira Teall,
a local tavern owner's young impetuous daughter, two centuries ago.
With the name came the City's impetuous vivacity—That early
impulsive desire to flirt with opportunity, and at times disaster.

Elmira, a beautiful name, the subject of a song or poem,
conjures up sepia-toned images of a mysterious woman.
Dark-featured, long black hair, and a youthful pouty smile.
While there, I sensed the air of mystery surrounding the city—A rare
blend of quantum energies, thrown off by its brutish industries
drawing life from the emotional Chemung River's waters.

Other stories, like the fabled Mark Twain's life in Elmira,
fills your head as you walk the City's streets and read its people.
Drawn by a beautiful woman named Olivia, Twain resided there on
and off for more than forty years, beginning just after the Civil War.
Some of his best works, including The Adventures of Huckleberry
Finn, were produced during summers at Elmira's Quarry Farm.

You learn a lot about an area when you pull out a scalpel
and perform open-heart surgery on its economy.
For one, names are important—People and places grow in and out
of names in interesting ways—Much as the story of Elmira goes,
making me wonder what the future holds for this river town named
after the impetuous tavern owner's daughter two hundred years ago.

Pittsburgh

Steel City.
City of bridges, where the waters
of the Allegheny, Monongahela, and Ohio converge, and
where old and new worlds meet.

Enterprising Pittsburgh glitters,
day and night from Mount Washington, and
from the Fort Pitt Tunnel—Sparkling downtown beckons
just across the mighty Monongahela.

A much admired symbol of the Industrial Heartland—
Its many stacks and chimneys belched rich sooty smoke.
Then the crucible of back-breaking, good-paying jobs, and
now a center of wealth-producing designs and new ideas.

Still a highly industrious urban center, but today
one built with clean advanced technologies.
A city of diverse global fortunes, and a place
where art, culture, and natural beauty commingle.

I grew up in the early '50s and '60s in eastern Ohio, and to me
Pittsburgh was the world's greatest city—A place we visited family,
and made regular pilgrimages to Forbes Field to see the Pirates play.
A big league city sparking man-size dreams in young boys.

It's little wonder Pittsburgh ranks so high
on my list of great American cities, and
it's perfectly understandable that Pittsburgh is
a city where enterprise truly thrives.

Tulare County

The name Tulare comes from "tules" in Spanish,
meaning reeds or cattails growing in marshes and wetlands.
460,000 people live in Tulare County, but as its residents quip,
the county has more cows than people—An observation validated
by the pungent bovine scent wafting across Highway 91.

Out-stretched at the feet of the Sierra Nevadas—
An inspiring visual landscape of mountain beauty.
An industrious place, people and businesses work productively.
Large busy dairy farms, the sound of cowbells in the morning fields.
Sprawling vineyards, a sweet grapey aroma all about.

Advantageous location within the San Joaquin Valley,
midpoint between Fresno and Bakersfield.
A leader in food production—Cheese, ice cream, and more.
Bustling distribution center with easy reach to coastal markets.
Finally, a growing regional tourism and healthcare center.

Back in 2002, I worked in Tulare County as a consultant—
Part of what the EDC's Paul Saldana called his "Dream Team"—
Four consultants hired to build the county's first economic strategy,
which we prepared working hand in hand with the communities of
Tulare, Exeter, Portersville, Dinuba, Visalia, and Lindsay.

I'm glad the past lingers in Tulare County—Indian rock art,
ghost towns, leave-behinds from pioneering gold rush days.
I love best the deep nature—the timeless wildflowers, streams, rolling
rocky fields, the sequoias, the ground-dwelling burrowing owl, and
last but not least the charismatic San Joaquin kit fox.

A place touches you deeply, if you open to its secrets—
Often overlooked in the economic development hustle bustle.
Tulare County left a lasting impression on my soul.
I wish for another trip back—
One more chance to sample Tulare's magic.

Economic Development Incentives

Some call incentives a necessary evil—
Every place everywhere seems to use them, and
they say it would be suicidal to unilaterally disarm.

For others, incentives are just evil—
Pure and simple corporate welfare.

Many see them as tools of the trade—
A worthy investment for business growth and jobs.

Some argue incentives are bad public policy—
Applying band aid solutions to ill-fated business tax policies.

Others contend incentives are intolerably unfair—
Favoring some businesses over others.

Then there are those crying out that incentives
are an unwise use of scarce public money, robbing
schools and communities of much needed revenues.

No matter what we think, we continue to use them
to sweeten deals, best the competition, and
line the pockets of already wealthy business owners.

My view? Outlaw them completely, or incentivize businesses
to create true broad-prosperity in communities.

Categorical Realities in Economic Development

Economic developers, like everyone else, make sense of the world
by putting things in categorical boxes, like existing business retention
and expansion and new business attraction.
Philosophers, and sometimes philosophical poets, remind us to
wrestle with the hard questions, and therefore we should ponder
whether our categorical boxes reflect reality.

Sense-making isn't easy—Just ask Aristotle,
who stayed up late many nights some 2,300 years ago,
creating formal categories he believed described reality.
Aristotle's ten major boxes were: substance, quantity, quality, relation,
place, being in a position, having, time, acting, and being acted upon.
And of course, each major box contains multiple subdivisions.

Economic developers have made good use of the Aristotelian boxes.
Businesses, communities, and jobs are all substances.
The number of jobs and size of a region's economy are quantities.
Place is used widely in economic development—We have our
neighborhoods, cities, counties, regions, and states.
And certainly everything we do has a time dimension.

You get my point—Economic developers are
avid Aristotelian box makers and users, and we are
proficient phylogeneticists, following in Carl Linnaeus' footsteps,
who published his 2,400-page *Systema Naturae* in 1768.
From Linnaeus, we borrowed the idea of corporate family trees,
industry clusters, and the very idea of evolutionary economics.

And I believe shortly, economic developers will apply
the DNA concept developed by Wilkins, Crick and Watson
to advance their categorical understanding of economic reality.
My only advice is that my friends keep in mind there is no biological
difference between a flower and a weed, leaving one to wonder
whether a weed is simply a flower in the wrong place.

Tucson

A sleepy tourist town back in 1969,
when I climbed off a Greyhound bus
on an unbearably hot early July afternoon
at the dusty bus station in downtown Tucson.

A growing place back then,
without much trying.
A community that continues to grow today,
but with much greater effort.

Originally dubbed the Old Pueblo
for its early Spanish origins.
Now a sprawling Western metropolis, stretched across
the Sonoran Desert into the surrounding mountain foothills.

Over one million people and a half a million jobs in the area today.
A thriving educational and healthcare center, with great impetus from
the fast-growing University of Arizona, with 40,000 students today
compared to 20,000 students when I enrolled there in 1969.

Known as the "Optics Valley" in light of the 150 local companies
designing and making optics and optoelectronic systems.
A burgeoning defense and advanced technology center.
A tourist mecca in winter with ample sunshine and glorious sunsets.

A place with great personal meaning to me,
sparking transformational lifetime friendships,
enduring connections to the desert and mountain beauty, and
opening doors to the ever-mysterious Native American world.

I still smile fondly, reflecting back on my younger days,
driving down Speedway in my red and white '54 Dodge,
the Beatles' Abbey Road album blaring from my 8-track tape deck.
Always a part of my heart will live in Tucson.

On Knowing the Future

Ancient Greece and Rome had their oracles, who with their crystal balls looked ahead. Communities today do much the same. Why the future dread? Some turn to consultants and others with subject matter expertise. Others work in-house with tea leaves, or data models scanning 360 degrees. I know many smart people working in economic development. Others I must say are like the blind men and the elephant. Local economies are forever in flux. No time when they stop moving and just stand still. As you can imagine, these changes cause businesses and communities to go up and downhill. For many years I prided myself as a good and worthy consultant. When I could truly help a client, I felt quite exultant. I once read a book by the philosopher J.M.E. McTaggart, who said the flow of time is an illusion, and time is really tenseless. I thought long and hard, and concluded his theory knocks all clocks senseless. If the determinists are right, there is little use in knowing a destiny you can't avoid. On the other hand, if we have free will, we can indeed fill the void. Bottom line to my economic development friends: Life is a gift to me. Accept your present, open it up, and you will surely see.

The Rise of the Spiritual Economy

Do businesses have souls? A question I've asked on occasion.
Perhaps that's why they set goals. A type of spiritual equation.
Businesses are alive. They are born and die.
Grow they must to survive. Never just standing by.

Ghosts in machines, animating workers' production.
Apparitions never demean. Reality a self-seduction.
These thoughts take aim at quantum understanding.
A world in which absolutely nothing is freestanding.

Several steps beyond 4-D printing, the quantum factory is born.
Robotic vestal virgins keep the fire. From its midst, a new unicorn.
A new economic reality lies ahead in the formless oceans.
Along with Schrödinger's cat and other quantum notions.

Tuck this poem away, but keep it close at hand.
On the horizon, a new economic promised land.
A place where the human mind will matter more than matter.
And without warning, the old-school capitalism mirror will shatter.

Sizing Right-Livelihood into Our Lives

At times, I become jaded
about the value of work
in bringing true meaning to people's lives.
Most of us work to survive—I get it.

Growing up in Eastern Ohio in the 1950s,
men literally killed themselves working—The area's unsafe
factories and coal mines maimed and killed many workers,
denying children of their fathers early on.

Today, fewer men and women die on the job, but
their work is still killing them—Stress and worry
live bullets in the working world's gun.
And for many, their life callings snuffed out by a job.

Economic developers see inside workplaces firsthand, and
they know the good and bad employers to work for.
Still too many low-wage/no-benefit jobs out there.
Modern slavery, in some towns still on the rise.

The worst thing is the broken spirits—Those losing hope
of getting ahead, a better life for their families.
Drugs in the workplace are a major problem, but work itself has
become an addictive drug, killing off the best parts of our lives.

The answer lies in balance—
Juggling those things most dear to our lives.
Let's hope the future brings a new type of rightsizing—
One aimed at sizing right-livelihood into our lives.

Shine Forth in Our Work

Our economic development work
should reflect our true spiritual essence.
Nothing more.
Nothing less.

We need a clean inner mirror
to see ourselves in our work.
Our true essence can then
shine forth to others.

We must practice reflecting upon
who we really are in our work.
Then there is no question whether
our work is meaningful.

On Economic Development Reality

Most of us try to live in reality. Yes, we try.
History is chock full of debates about the nature of reality.
Several generations of philosophers have exhausted
thousands of midnight candles on the subject.

Reality is a topic of discussion in our everyday lives.
In my own work, I am struck by the number of times
boards of directors, executives, news reporters, and others
get tangled up in arguments over the nature of reality.

How many times have I heard the question: "What are my
community's real economic development strengths?"
And how many times have I heard the statement:
"We need to get real!"

I concluded some years ago, after much pain and suffering,
that reality is not as easy as it seems—for any of us.
And that's exactly why I love John Lennon's observation:
"Reality leaves a lot to the imagination."

Managing

In the absence of control, we must manage.
Change is the only constant, we navigate by managing.
Organization is only space on the artist's canvas.
Everybody paints on the canvas, not just owners and managers.
Management is not a job or profession, rather
it is a moral commitment to adapt—
A commitment that evolves moment by moment,
step by step, and person by person.
We must manage.

Producing What Matters

Imagine a city,
filled with factories,
producing only love.

Picture the world,
connected by vast trade networks,
exchanging only joy.

See your job,
inspired by music, art, and nature,
bringing happiness to yourself and others.

Love, joy, art, nature, happiness.
These are the things
that really matter.

Building Economic Labyrinths

Too often we see life as a puzzle to be solved—That's what happens
when we talk with too many bankers and engineers.
Try talking with artists and poets—Life turns into a labyrinth,
that is a path of meaning to be experienced.
The labyrinth teaches us that end points, looked at properly,
become new beginning points—Places allowing us to start over, and
places offering us new vantage points, allowing us
to see ourselves and the world differently.
Think of your community's economic path, not as a roadmap,
but as a labyrinth—A path of discovery, rebirth, and rejuvenation.

Leadership

Better leadership, folks say,
is what we need
to become greater,
not just in economic development,
but in everything.

What is leadership?
Is it the noun leadership,
meaning the right people to lead?
Is it the verb leadership,
meaning right actions taken by leaders?

We need both:
Leadership as a noun and verb.
But for me, the starting point is self-leadership:
Doing a better job leading our own lives, and
putting the best of ourselves out in front.

Sacred Cows and Sacrificial Lambs

Sacred cows, what we won't give up.
Not that Holstein, Jersey, or Hereford, but
how about your beef with city council, or
that cow you had over losing that investment deal?

Maybe it's those professional masks
we allow our egos to paint on our faces.
Perhaps it's those tired old stories we tell
about why things can't change.

Sacrificial lambs, what we give up,
instead of what we should give up.
Could be anything we don't care much about—
Except our sacred cows.

Maybe it's someone we throw under the bus
to make a powerbroker like us, or perhaps
it's a token change we make in ourselves to convince
others we are giving and caring human beings.

Sacred cows, what we protect
to keep ourselves from changing.
Sacrificial lambs, what we surrender
to keep ourselves from changing.

Small Towns Down on Their Luck

So many small towns—
Desperate.
Down on their luck.
Fallen, unable to get back up.
No way to revive opportunity.

I've seen their faces—
all those left behind, young and old,
losing it all, including their dreams.
Gone, more than they ever imagined.
Prosperity, a vanishing ghost,
leaving folks cold and empty.

Times are tough in many small places—
Despite larger economic gains.
I believe hope is still out there,
but wrapped in unfamiliar clothes.
We need a new consciousness—
To see and then act differently.

The Karmic Wheel

That overlooked, we become.
Tracks us down, like a hungry wolf.
Eventually catching up, devours us.
Leaving nothing, but itself.

That forgotten, returns.
Haunting us, night and day.
When least suspected, it floods back.
Taking with it, all we protect.

That which we pretend to be
engraves its name upon us
for all to see what we have become, and
what we are no longer.

And so turns the karmic wheel
around and around
until at last
its work with us is done.

Cleveland Looking Back and Ahead

I have proudly lived in the Cleveland area since 1972, and while
at times I have had my doubts about the City and the region,
the area has been very good to me, my family, career, and life in
general—I am grateful for the gifts and opportunities it has given me.

Cleveland and Northeast Ohio have had their ups and downs—
From Best Location in the Nation to the Mistake on the Lake.
Fighting back from the brink, Cleveland's greatness gene is birthing
new foundational opportunities for the City and the region.

Downtown, University Circle, the lakefront, the Euclid Corridor, and
many neighborhoods have stronger heartbeats today, but progress
must be sustained and hastened, touching more ordinary people,
lifting them up with greater hope and prosperity.

The Cavaliers ended Cleveland's national championship drought,
besting the Warriors, winning the 2016 NBA title, and a month later,
Cleveland hosted a successful Republican National Convention,
sparking greater confidence in and praise for the City.

Much work lies ahead—I believe our leadership gets it, but
they need our help, especially everyone's willingness to work together
to build something great for the future—A community where
people take care of themselves and each another.

While Cleveland must continue to win and grow pride, the bigger job
goes beyond winning—We must convert our victories into conscious
evolution and true resilience, and we must turn our pride into
gratitude—the greatest competitive advantage for the future.

When Singularity Reaches Economic Development

Singularity is a hypothesized future, where super-intelligent machines
play a much greater role in all affairs of work and life.
From what I hear, this future is closer at hand—
And science-fiction is morphing into science.

What will we do when singularity reaches economic development,
and robots plot to take over the jobs of economic developers?
Should we take our place in the unemployment line, or should
we weigh in now on the code written for these genius machines?

Take solace my fellow professionals in knowing
that Isaac Asimov has our backs
with his three laws of robotics,
set out in *Runaround*, published in 1943.

Applied to economic development,
Asimov's laws of robotics are these:
First, a robot may not injure an economic developer, or
through inaction allow an economic developer to come to harm.

Second, a robot must obey orders given it by an economic developer,
except where such orders conflict with the first law.
Third, a robot must protect its own existence, as long as such
protection does not conflict with the second and third laws.

But in the event Asimov's laws are overturned by the Supreme Court,
the International Economic Development Council should develop a
new training program preparing economic developers and their
robots to work together in harmony in advancing local economies.

A Good Economic Developer

A good economic developer is
self-aware and aware of others,
learns from others and teaches others,
sees the big and small pictures,
exhibits authenticity and honesty,
anticipates and adapts to change,
acts in line with vision and knowledge,
works with passion and compassion,
accepts responsibility for his/her actions,
tolerates ambiguity and complexity,
seeks and brings about simplicity,
germinates and tolerates diversity,
brings about inclusivity,
builds shared understanding,
meets today's needs, and
prepares for tomorrow's needs,
exhibits professional skills and knowledge,
balances the needs of economy and community,
and leads from the front and behind.

Finally, a good economic developer
does the right thing,
in the right way,
at the right time,
for the right reason.

And when these things fail,
a good economic developer
should reach into his pocket,
pull out his sense of humor,
and recall the words of Francis Bacon:
"Imagination was given to man
to compensate him for what he is not, and a
sense of humor to console him for what he is."

The Economic Development Color Wheel

The world is mostly gray.
Rarely black and white.
And very often,
it is an ever-changing rainbow.

Truth is a color wheel
we spin and spin
until we get
the color we want.

On the surface
we spin economic development
as jobs and prosperity
for ordinary people in communities.

Below the surface
economic development is
more green and gold
for the wealthiest and most powerful.

Economic development rides the color wheel
until the power brokers say
stop we like this color, or
spin the wheel some more.

What is your favorite color?

The South Wheeling Sylvania Electric Plant Closing in 1967

I was a sophomore in high school in 1967, when
Sylvania Electric shuttered operations in South Wheeling,
throwing my father and seventy other workers into the streets.
This was my first personal encounter with economic development.

To support us, Dad took a menial job at an industrial laundry,
which paid half his earnings at Sylvania—but a job for which
he was grateful, but Mom never forgave Sylvania Electric
for what she called a kick-in-the-teeth to working families.

Dad frequently told the story about John F. Kennedy's visit
to the South Wheeling Sylvania Electric Plant in April 1960.
A rare opportunity for the factory and workers to shine, and yet
it wasn't enough to prevent what happened seven years later.

The South Wheeling plant closing was part of a much larger
economic shift—just the beginning of the unraveling of the Ohio
Valley's economic base, as coal, steel and other manufacturing jobs
declined in the face of new technologies and foreign competition.

Unable to find a summer job in 1969 after high school graduation,
I left the Ohio Valley—Never to return to live again, and
one year later my family followed suit.
Arizona put us all back on our feet—jobs, education, and more.

Would my family have stayed in the Ohio Valley if the
Sylvania plant hadn't closed? I'd say no—
More opportunity, a brighter future in other places.
Same decision we would have made.

Today we have no family living in the Ohio Valley, and
truly that is a shame, for families get attached to places.
And yet, people must take care of themselves, while
working on a new American Dream

Ashtabula City

Proudly poised on the river and the lake.
A port city—a unique opening to the universe.
Over time, a gathering place for industry and commerce, and
just as importantly, a place where people live,
and their spirits call home.
A place with deep living roots—
those you can feel as well as see
on this chilly early November morning.
There is a tempo to places, like Ashtabula—
a music that gets etched into our souls, and
Ashtabula has a natural rhythm—
something utterly divine imbued in
everything we see and touch.
Despite its problems,
the world is a beautiful place, and
Ashtabula is a beautiful city—
a one-of-a-kind painting, still wet
with life and color.

Ashtabula County

Ashtabula County has a poetry—
A creative way of expressing who it is through
its urban and rural places, hardworking and caring people,
and its scenic beauty, landscapes, and vast open spaces.

Ashtabula's Bridge Street overflowing in summer—
Partying people honoring wine, walleye and more.
In the background, the unrelenting bascule lift bridge,
up and down every half hour for boaters and fun makers.

Conneaut's D-Day reenactments of the amphibious Allied landings
upon the beaches of Normandy—A stark reminder
of the anguish and beauty of the Big War, replayed every August
in the City's harbor and along the lakeshore.

Covered bridges, fly-fishing, and scenic rivers,
Factory towns like Orwell, tourist destinations like Geneva,
Harbors, lake freighters, coal trains, and blinking lighthouses—
All find their places in the vast stretches of Ashtabula County.

Diverse economic base, holding its own day to day,
Producing milk, growing grapes, corn, and Miscanthus grass,
Molding and extruding plastic and rubber products,
and brewing complex chemicals and colorful coatings.

In sleepy Jefferson, the red brick county courthouse, and around
the town, factories, fields, and freshly painted fences and houses.
On Sunday mornings, hear angelic voices sing in South County's
Amish churches, then stroll the picturesque Andover Square.

Ashtabula County—Self-reliant, resourceful, low-key by nature,
So much you find, from subtle tinkling cowbells in springtime,
to the deafening quiet deep snows of winter to the music and parties
on hot summer nights in downtown Geneva on the Lake.

What's Next After Forty Years in Economic Development?

No regrets on my choice of a professional career.
I love life even more as retirement draws near.
Like most everyone else, I'm shocked how fast life flies by.
Wakes me up nights with a deep gasp and long sigh.

So many lessons about life I've learned from my work.
Things I never expected, not a one I would ever shirk.
Despite the ups and downs over the years.
I'm glad I stayed in the field and never shifted gears.

I've loved the people, the urban and rural places.
Equally so, the wild open spaces.
In gratitude to others who brought me much good.
On shoulders of giants I surely have stood.

Hopefully wisdom and love comes with the years.
And laughter, thanksgiving, a few joyous tears.
To write and teach others now is my passion.
Poetry for one flows in high fashion.

My job at this point is to open the door for others.
Celebrate my economic development sisters and brothers.
This book is the start of new things to come.
The better I hope the world will become

ABOUT THE AUTHOR

Don Iannone is an economic developer, poet, writer, teacher and photographer who lives in Cleveland, Ohio with his wife Mary and their three calico cats. Don has two grown sons, Jeffrey and Jason, and one grandson, Evan.

After nearly forty years in the local economic development field, Don has decided that poetry and philosophy have something to offer economic development, and he went to work on *Poetic and Philosophical Reflections on Economic Development*, his fourth book of poetry. It follows on the heels of *Chasing Cosmic Butterflies*, his third poetry book, which was published earlier in 2016. Don is also the author of five photography books.

Don's economic development career includes working for a regional planning and development organization, metropolitan chamber of commerce, two countywide economic development organizations, a state university, and since 2000 he has run his own economic development consulting company.

Don completed an undergraduate degree in Anthropology at Cleveland State University, graduate studies in Organizational Behavior at Case Western Reserve University, a professional diploma from the Economic Development Institute at the University of Oklahoma, and an M.A. degree in Consciousness Studies from the University of Philosophical Research in Los Angeles, where he currently teaches essay writing.

Don's website: http://www.donaldiannone.com

Wisdom Work Press: https://wisdomworkpress.wordpress.com